Original Human

Original Human

Poems by Deborah DeNicola

Word Press

Published by Word Press
P.O. Box 541106
Cincinnati, OH 45254-1106

ISBN: 9781936370207
LCCN: 2010942169

Poetry Editor: Kevin Walzer
Business Editor: Lori Jareo

Visit us on the web at www.word-press.com

Acknowledgments

Awakened Woman: "Bronze Goddess Speaks"
Bloodlotus: "The Gospel of Mary"
Buttonwood Press Review: "Transfiguration on Mt. Tabor,"
        "Magdalen"
California Quarterly: "Mid-Morning" (as "Delicious")
Cortland Review: "Dusk"
Crab Orchard Review: "Theresa in Ecstasy"
Cross Currents: "Ascension Thursday,"
Dogwood: "Early Childhood"
Ekphrasis: "Van Gogh's Room," "Doorway at Lake Como,"
        "Bethany"
Falling Rain: Anthology: "Fool" (one section of "Tarot")
Family Reunion: Anthology: "Visual Ritual"
Fort Point: "October Stars"
Green Mountain Review: "I Was Looking Into Your Eye," "Mystique"
Hunger Mountain: "When He Said"
Jabberwock Review: "Final Longitude"
Lalitamba Journal: "Moment"
Louisville Review: "Kafka's '*Metamorphosis,*' as "The Saddest Story"
Main Channel Voices: "The Preponderance of the Small"
The North American Review: "Gauguin's Red"
Off Channel: "Eve, Eons After" as "The Glass Darkly"
Orion: "This Morning From The Porch," "Last Judgment"
Ousamequin: "Tree"
Pif Magazine: "In The Valley of the Shadow"
Pemmican: "Crow"
Polyphony: "Rouen 1431"
Psychological Perspectives: "The Hour Done"
Runes: "First Trip to the Infinite"
Salamander: "Hanging Man" (one section of *"Tarot"*)
Second Glance: "Jesus to Judas, From Kingdom Come"
The King's English: "Hair By Hair" and "Only One Remark More"
Tonopah Review: "Self-Portrait With Parents."

Twenty-one poems in this manuscript appeared in *The Harmony of the Next* which won the Riverstone Press Chapbook Award, 2005. Eighteen poems appeared in the chapbook *Inside Light* from Finishing Line Press, 2007. "I Am, I Will" won the 2009 Santa Barbara Poetry Award. "John Baptizing Jesus" won The William T. Foley Award and appeared in *America,* 2000. "This Morning From the Porch" and "Theresa in Ecstasy" won the 1995 and 1993

Barbara Bradley Award from The New England Poetry Club. "Hair By Hair" received a Pushcart Prize nomination, 2004. "Tuesday Night With The I Ching" first appeared in *Psyche Revisited*, which won the 1992 Embers Chapbook Contest.

The epigram before "The Oracle of the Body" is from *Zero Gravity* by Eric Gamalinda, Alice James Books, 1998. The epigram before "Original Human" is from *Eros & Chaos: The Sacred Mysteries and Dark Shadows of Love* by Veronica Goodchild, Nicholas Hays, 2001.

I am grateful to the National Endowment for the Arts for a poetry fellowship that gave me time for some of these poems. Many thanks to friends and colleagues, Alan Albert, Anne Fowler, Barbara Helfgott-Hyett, Margaret Holley, Kurt Leland, The Monday Group and The Charles River Poets Workshop for their help with feedback.

Table of Contents

I
Oracles

II
Worlds

III
Edens

*Lord, we know what we are, but not
what we may be.*

—Ophelia

I
Oracles

Ascension Thursday

Out the plane's porthole at thirty-thousand feet,
ascension looks almost do-able.
A royally cubited arc falls
like a stairwell from clouds,
and I could puncture the plugged muffle
of voices across the aisle, ululate
a Hildegarde revival

if I cared to. Otherwise,
with my hundred eighty-seven
milliliters of wine, I'm going to
give off a cabernet glow

from pineal gland to root sensor
where blossoms of subtler bodies rise—
After the *little while,*
when they'd *see me no longer,*

I too would come back for my friends,
unveil the roads to the kingdoms
within them, ripening even the worst
of the people we know. In a room

of ecru linen, I'd let loose a few
beneficent doves just as the sun spangled
our pearled terra firma, just as
it swiveled the fuse of our circle low,
just grazing our hair—

while we'd watch one another dissolve
into the godspell to which we'd been
called, bewildered, but gifted—surely
delivered, surely converting
to light.

Rouen, 1431

Jeanne d'Arc

Old victory stales,
ebbs to a new field

of blood. Voices
gone, all

reinforcements contracted
in the wrong light,

the breath of heaven
heaving elsewhere

as the Dauphin
in the damask chair

lifts his pinkie
for more fruit and

fuchsia wine. Behind
these dungeon doors

my moat of words,
sealed—on the wrong side

of evil, my secrets,
spilt grails among

unbelievers. Stripped
of armor, horse and hair,

passed to these priests,
their black hoods, their

candelabrum haunts,
their big books,

I see there is *nothing*
to do with truth—

Voices gone, my cries
bore god . . . my whispers

Vive La France!
All inner fire, white-

cindered, white-
calcined, *blanc*—

Magdalen

*(The Disciples) said to him, 'Why do you love her more than all of us?' The Savior
answered and said to them, "Why do I not love you like her?"* —The Gospel of Philip

History named me a whore.
But history fears women
with power

and finds an excuse. I was worse.
The Sorceress of Magdala, I knew
the patterns of imbalance
which horn beam cured.
Tranquility induced by larch and beech.

Stirring palliatives of aspen and clematis
in a slow boil of weeds, I mixed elixirs for dropsy
and warts. When I taught, I taught throats to open,
intoning the centers along the spine
and I knew chants

to extract the animal rage from a lover.
Thomas called me the thirteenth apostle,
unlucky, and Peter wanted me gone.
But Christ knew me as kin, knew history
would be unkind. After the crowd broke up
that night, we sat and talked on my pallet,

my elbow brushed his as I shared the figs
hidden under my cloak. Our burden came clear
in the first taste of fruit. Even the air circling our limbs
slid into contours like caresses, each glow
weaving the other's shadow. Dark blew out the sky
and only the fire of our doubled ethers lit up the hut.

The method of love is not as important as its transmission.
And how bad is it for the gospel's infamous slut,
if the soul lives her purpose? If the heart that has learned
to transcend—then, transcends?

Theresa In Ecstasy

after the sculpture by Giovanni Bernini

Bernini's beatific
mystic—humility's folds
tucked into her robe

like the tubercular vow
caught in her lung.

To martyr the self in its rash imperfection
is an urgency no virgin would know.

But Theresa's the *bride* of Christ
flown into trance, mantle flung back,

violet eyelids
low and euphoric, fluttery
tensing of fingers and toes,
fever

blessing her muscles,
oxygen fog in her blood,
bones strung

in loose modulation
like notes of Gregorian chant,
a hum off the moon

as the voice of the Spouse
sails down through the bell-
shaped shadows

where her raised index finger
trembles
inside the marble

and molecules swoon
through lavender-pure
and murmuring
stone.

John Baptizing Jesus

He must have been a sight,
      barbaric hair, dilated eyes—(prelude
         to Herodias' still life on the platter—)

They say he lived on wild honey and the long torsos
      of locusts, that he dressed in fetid camel pelts
         and rags—and that he ranted

as if he had a finger in a messianic
      socket, his arm, a limb of lightning
         in the shallows of the Jordan.

Then one day Jesus in his yellow hair. The whole head
      thundering under water, and heaven downloaded
         between the bodies of two cousins,

baptist and carpenter,
      genetic tripwires sizzling—the Holy Spirit
         furring vision, and then the Lord's voice—

great blue whale
      beached on the banks of being. Rose light
         on the mountains, all mythic harvest—sheen

and mystery, all potential in the instantaneous
skating of the clouds, then *recognition*
         as the boys, wet and electric,

nod to one another the unremitting readiness, the *Now*—
      And the ecstatic knowing.
         The tragic ecstatic knowing.

Eve, Eons After

It was like the genie effect.
We were sucked into a hole
at the lower left of the garden.

I wanted to know the opposite
of Eden—to compare in order to love more
what we had. *No*—I am already lying,

sinning against the gift. The thought
to separate from God was immediate,
an unraveling, imagining something other

than beauty. Now grief, now guilt,
abstractions I couldn't name before.
Where orchids once were

perfect, all color gone. In their place
angry weeds and torched fields. We fell
into the abysmal, walls grew mountainous,

spiked rocks underfoot where once
was grass. Here it rains shame. Night
goes on all hours, dims my thoughts

of dirty chores that call off morning.
Adam stares and sleeps like a book
with pages missing. I can't recall

the sky-scent of daylight, the shade
of the olive branch. I am naked, deep
in my torn aura. We asked for this

and then forgot. Eden, hidden now
behind the veil that fell. Or so
we think . . . and thought creates—

the glass darkly.

Bronze Goddess Speaks

Sequana, Gallo-Romain

There is too much woundedness out the window and inside
the TV where guards secure this blank room. Too much
pain trickling from the faucet in the toilette where water
will be the next thing these poor humans horde.
I can see from my boat they are a sad lot, and sinking.
In 5000 years, life after life, no one has learned a thing

about love. It is a fine ideal for me to sit in the archeological
museum in Dijon, the stillness sanctioned by the embalmed
air. Still, I am here to overhear prayers and inspire new histories.
But even as legions pass, their thoughts flare in my hooded eyes
like 20th century weapons. Their tears deliver so much salt
each morning, birds convulse in the summer heat while insects

evolve new powers. Men scarcely stop to look me over,
still, their hunger resonates like song lines through rocks
and soil. One young woman craves love, another success.
One dreadful girl begs for peace so quietly she doesn't hear
the scream in her voice, while all the Mother's estranged
daughters request the courage to bear the world.

Because I am ancient, most show respect, yet some
would just as soon trade me on the black market.
Still others believe I can help and those help themselves
by believing. Whether I listen, or not—is beside the point.
Belief is the point, though I am no longer what they believe in
and so tired of soaking up wishes like oils from Roman baths.

Dug up from earth, once I was charged terra but lost all strength
when wrenched from my pagan well, one of hundreds
beneath the land where Gothic Cathedrals were built.
What I know continues unchanged but changes nothing.
If only they knew how powerful the earth, how free they are
to love it—they might stop punishing themselves.

Vanitas

Sunflowers loll in these fields outside Aix
shading the gothic churches of these southern
provinces where all figures of Mary Magdalene,
whether pigment or stone, hold a skull in one hand.
Lounging bone of the brow, the proud jaw as a gruesome

basket, remind us we will surely be spaded and ground
to ash. So what does luxuriant flesh suggest? The notion
the mind believes—*the body is all*—is *us?* Not *over* us,
not us inside? Once as a girl growing up in the desert
I watched buzzards overhead and thought of that slow

transmutation to slate, to sand. Now I kneel
before my own aging image. Under a lowered rheostat
in tinted glass, I attempt to love the loosening sackcloth
of skin, the scaffold beneath my face. Dear Jesus,
let me love myself as I am—the way you loved

both of the Marys—and everyone else for the light
within. And Lord, if it helps, I can think of the body
as the digested shank of the lamb, or the deboned fish,
or the misconstrued shell, pierced and appended

to an olivewood cross. The flesh as something misleading,
like the tinseled pentagram above a Renaissance icon,
something finite and false. A medieval Pardoner's relic,
some saint's fingernail, its glowing luster of abalone,
the human body, more matter than art, a rip-off, silly—.

Numerology

And there, amidst the abstraction
of a universal code, I began to read
the future from medieval history,
to gauge the sacred shapes of geometry
which could carry me to the quantum
leap of the heart matching that flower
in the sky, the giant star the Egyptians
psychoanalyzed, for it was always
the sun, those volleys of braggadocio
which illuminated morning,
circumambulating a globe
colored by numbers . . .

If I must remain face down in the dirt
of the earth spelling darkness ten different ways,
then let the integers steer the light
let them measure the ultra-violets,
magnetic pores and portals,
let heat and conductivity begin.

Mt. Tabor

Matthew 17:1-8

Dizzy from the Palestinian taxi,
above the bowl of sanded vistas,
my mother and I recalled how Jesus
took Peter, John and James
and walked up this very mountain
stepping through sky,

to dazzle the disciples with his altered
state—long hair haloed,
robe kindled in gold,
and how Moses and Elijah stepped
from the fan of flames,

so that three men made of light
spoke as if on a street-corner
leaning on lampposts—

while the apostles gaped . . .
Peter babbling on about pitching tents
for their unexpected guests . . .

*

My mother stood a long time
in her imagined sins, pages
of her prayer book leafing in the breeze,
while I moved deeper in through the weight

of my body, then out beyond
the mountain's crest. Fixed
on the point of a sword-like cloud,
I walked the plank of my own
unorthodox belief and did not scold myself

for the thought that I was part of God.
I went spinning out and out,
leaving my head and trunk

on the escarpment, went out and back
to the prelapsarian ungendered *All.*
For several seconds I was *gone* . . .

*

Afterwards, I kept silent, told no one,
because when Moses and Elijah left
the radiant vapor of their cloud,
Christ returned to his own dense flesh
and said to his stunned friends:
Tell No One What You've Seen This Day

as they followed him through scrub
and haze all afternoon, hiking
back down the lilied footpath of Tabor
and on to supper with the others
in the blue breadbasket of Jezreel.

The Shadow of The Valley

First night with no moon. Heat so deep
it sucks a Bedouin oasis. Dead Sea,
perfectly still where Jesus stands.

Satan paces behind him—Snake-oil spokesman
for illusion, *You can be richer, stronger*—
Us against Them he says, and Jesus lets him
talk awhile, for awhile even listens.
His breath scalds like a smoke of moths—

but he's not above his shadow's fears
and weeps at his vision, Jerusalem's
burning, the garrison looting, skewering
children. He knows Satan wants him
weak when he offers Caesar's kingdom.

When Christ looks down, he dangles sorrow
over limestone, fashioning a city out of air—
Lately wavelengths with his other world
have been erratic, channels jammed, currents
crossed and that image of that crucifix, nothing
he cares to look at. The demon laughs,

sputum flies, brush fires brew where it lands
and rodents gallop—*You're not real unless I say so*
Jesus answers and Satan flares his bat cape,
spinning off the parapet to fall like dust
on Jesus's sandal. Ash and bone
spaded by sun. The sulfurous scent

of wires shorting out.
Christ stumbles on his shelf of shale,
whispers *Be Gone—my troubled twin,*
Oh withered angel—Lost semblable,
forgiving the dark part of himself.

Bethany

Mary Magdalene in Stained Glass, Rennes-le-Chateau.

I was wiping his feet with my hair
when I heard Judas snicker
over the salve. The spikenard, the pungent

scent, the expense. Christ waved him
away, scolded his calculation,
that paltry sum. What jewel, what gem

or silver could steady the scale?
I let my fingers travel and they cried out,
racing circles in small figure eights

on top of each foot . . . Oh,
the moons of the toes, those
pale nails—his worn skin like crepe-

everlasting. Though he shared
the intricacies of the pact with me alone,
I wanted his body intact. My hair

hid my tears, the way smoked clouds
hide rain. We are circumscribed
on this earthen stone. Noosed in our own

Uroborus—What we knew was incomplete.
What is destiny next to the body's love?
The hair on my neck

stood up at the thought
of the olive grove, the centurion's
severed ear. And how does one face

the climax of what one desired
so much—oh the wash, the rubbing
unguent. *Just touch*—such as it is
on this serpentine rock.

Noli Me Tangere

There was a presence before the stone.
A pressure so much larger than human
wounds. My mind let go into the crags
of sorrow and I grew
this cavernous heart. It was a tomb
but also a garden. One is the other
always. The spirit rises. The body stays
and blooms. I took him
for the gardener as the roses were wilted
on the lattice near where he stood.
He'd been broken and nailed
but nothing showed. Not one thorn,
not one bruise. The light stunned,
and magnetized me reaching for his robe.
He threw out his arm, bolt
of lit wires—shocked—I fell back.
 And how removed he was, glowing
from his brow, both palms. No seams
for the ravaged flesh. The shade of white
on his garment, almost golden
like the air behind his head
when he taught us *Truth:*
No one dies. No one
ever dies. No one is alone.
The painters only saw my body
as pulp, pigment and bone, the thick
color of my hair. But I was traveling
without movement, statue-still,
hardly there while all my being
hummed. He said my name
and my head knocked inside
the sky. The suns in his eyes
burned through. I came to myself
stupefied, not knowing when he'd gone.
And I ran to tell the brothers
we must *choose* belief, despite the fears
which fool our senses, the fear
which covered Eden up.

Tuesday Night With The I Ching

The oracle answers my inquiry with the hexagram
Deliverance. I see a runway the length of God.
A platter of sublime and milky light
before the sleek shadow of a plane lifts off
above relentless ocean, grids
of land-locked fields and tilted houses—

above the conflict the ancients tell me to deny.
The one that picks and picks at the granite quarry,
a committed Sisyphus, running up, running down.
Alright, I surrender to *deliverance*
like a samurai accepts the risk of his noble death,
in defense of a crown. Death by dragon,
by fire-walking, the brandished edge
of the sword, the cliff, and sky

so lucid and blue—consciousness
gathers its essence like flavors
brewed in a delicate cup
and escapes the body. *Deliverance*
is an act of the will giving up the will
as its only option. *Paradox*

as orientation to some sacred sunrise
where a bird steps out of the dawn
and walks with the long-legged yak
across a Himalayan palette, strewing
gold footprints over the ridges—

Deliverance is the future unspoken,
unwritten, the late morning fog
pressing its imprint atop Mount Everest—

the highest peak in Tibet,
the hardest path.

Jesus to Judas From Kingdom Come

Go and do quickly that which you must do.

John 13:27

It's true. Though the others never recorded it in their texts,
I loved him best and knew from the moment we met he would
require something more to pull off his business—Nights on the road,
between miracles, I would catch him watching me with beady eyes
as if he might steal my bag of tricks, pull a pigeon from a flap

in our tent, expose a mirror from the pocket of my robe. It's easy
to worship blindly. And there was a balance struck between
the believing naif and the Roman cynic; few had that hairline down
like he did—Distracted from my teaching, always pushing the limits
of what could be known hands-on, fingering coins, correct change

in the market, or retrieving ledgers Matthew kept for taxes (his
wine-swigging the night of the wedding . . .) And he took inordinate
time checking the count of the fishes—choosing the tangible over
what must remain abstract, not like the shade of a man's skin,
but the shape of prayer, the texture of sin, as if one could measure

Satan's gloss in the desert at noon when the sun splayed the horizon.
He lacked that fusion, dust on an eyelash, that feel for a fourth
dimension. With his long fingers he'd pluck at his red beard, flash
a disarming question, forehead compressed, mouth crimped down
in sullen resistance to the simplicity of the word *love* . . . So I grew

certain I could trust him to carry out the plan. And he knew I knew,
after supper, after I washed his gnarly feet, after I stroked his hand,
understanding within an hour in the garden, still with the bloody
wine on his breath, he would dispatch the final piece. Not with silver,
but with the kiss, that tenuous kiss, how I dreamt it and dreaded it.

I relied on him, on his mind that could not go beyond our human
significance—Yet I regret that we never acknowledged the mutual
set-up, that I never thanked him in the flesh as I looked down
through the storm, watching his spirit rise just ahead of me—
And I blessed both earthly bodies hanging from their respective trees.

Last Judgment
after Rilke

In togas, in rags, in gowns of falling flesh, disorderly
they kneel, they supplicate, they squat. They gather in plazas,
on playgrounds, on the commons, not to be distracted
from their prayer, which they have found themselves

like a lake of loons and pines, inside of.
Then angels come, begin their renovation,
magnetic plasma honing throats to speak belief—
dispatching the actual gods of themselves toward wish,

toward trust—those reliquaries deep in the solar plexus,
dousing the fiery fields where fear is eaten whole by risk.
And the only judgment comes when fear looks back

on the world it made, appalled—as wild roses rise
from the parking lots. As if to say *We grow—*
That's what we do. *We've been here all along.*

The Oracle of The Body

Coagulated dust, Colorado rock
flood the instep of my boots.
Cattle low to roots of trees and quartz
which lie like a neuron network
in the lap of mountains. Something
stirs the sagebrush. The cows themselves,
without reflection, step aside,
sensing the presence passing through.

I follow, drawn but aimless in the limited
light of all I know, when the oracle
calls forth from visible earth
invisible bodies, light as the birds
I share the air with. I willingly
empty my mind of objects, thoughts,
emotion, and turn like a naked Francis
to feed stray apparitions,
shedding the cloth of manmade
world. I share the poverty that gives

as if from that bottomless basket
where bread and fish made manifest
the clear intention of a man who read
in the sunset a synchronous heaven
and earth—Yet I have learned nothing
worshiping him, instead of becoming

the *love* that he is, amongst those
who "will do these things also—"
The numen of those who vanish where
more light holds, births a door
in my forehead, a gnosis of new senses
sending up my blood and bone,
this land of manure and mud

while my body conducts the core
and I open my palms to the earth I am
under the lavender bowl of sky, under all
that is given freely, far from the careless slaughter,
far from the urban confusions—the border
of northern New Mexico
here at the ranch on the edge.

For Mark Irwin

Tarot

> *Though their purses shrank, their souls gained in stature.*
> —C. G. Jung

Hanging Man

All my earth reversed in an instant. As if I stepped
on the nerve of the universe—can never return
to leveled view. Strung by one welted ankle,
here surrender is more than survival, *absolute,*
almost virtue. What did I know erect,
but the cage of myself?

Magician

I know the game. Breath, flint, spark and a fired seed,
I contain all possibilities in my hat. An egg, a rod,
a drop of water. Syzygy through space,
the drive of sap through branches—my release,
is simply mana. Call me the unborn who emerges
out of nothing. I purify the cauldron, coin the lead.
Go ahead—Ask me to resurrect your wasted world.

Hermit

I carry my own light out of the hypnagogic gloom.
No sun, or star—Still, my bare beam opens direction.
Flanked by forests, cloaked from contact, I stoop
on my staff. Birds drop berries, secrets
that seal this path from evil. How the nights
are patient—tamping my thoughts.

Fool

The unnumbered, *zed, void, squat*—I'm out
of the loop—no name or home, one of the passive
poor. Nowhere and everywhere, treading the air
to the first heaven. Buds blossom when I pass,
hobo bundle on my back, ferrying my pilgrimage
to the 10,000 things. I have nothing to do
but ascend.

Doorway at Lake Como

after the photograph by Jay Kaufman

It's one of so many Medieval doorways
studded with iron and green men, cornucopia
heavier than alchemical lore. A cursed treasure
within, perhaps under brickwork, fleur-de-lis burnt
into the hearth. Some lesser holy of holies
folded into a strong box the color of rust.
Sepia light as collective memory,
a half dozen skulls strung together with chains,
and multi ex-votos gracing the walls. Some knight's

broken visor nearby. An owl and gargoyle
sculpted into the arch beg for nightmare—Imagine
a Templar mystic in soot-stained cape skulking beneath
fallen starlight. Lifting one scuffed boot to the threshold,
spitting a code at the slot, he genuflects backwards,
descends coughing into the crypt. Stolen remains
of crusaders, their ashes now swept with those
at the stakes, far from the waters the brothers swam
off Isle de Côte, baked bones in their teeth.

The Gospel of Mary

My brother Peter, Do you think that I thought this up myself or that I am lying about the Savior?—The Gospel of Mary

I was not alarmed when the doves continued to coo
though their wings were burning.

I was on fire too.
It was morning. I was there

with the eleven. We were gathered
in the vestibule of the upper room.

Our breath thickened, colors deepened.
For just one instant I saw the root of love

staked through the ceiling. But so few of them
received the vision at its core.

They tried to *think* it through. It was not
for thought. It was more

for holding and becoming. Light
brandished from our fingertips

like swords of warrior angels.
When it extinguished,

I flashed my ordinary hands
and we all laughed.

Because they asked, I told them
what he said to me in private,

I didn't say he'd kissed me
on the mouth. I told them how

I met the savior *inside* my head.
How our thoughts entwined

like bean stalks
through swatches of clouds.

How he said *thought*
created matter, and *fear*

is ingenious for damaging the world.
He said *Here is the soul, here the Spirit,*

the mind—
a naive child between them.

I drew a diagram in air of the soul's
escalation, my fingers sparking

the seven heavens. I tried to show
what rushes naked, leaving the body

like a town one no longer cares to visit.
How the soul, small and homeless,

remembers then, and rejoins Spirit.
How, in the aftermath, oblivion

is transient, and darkness is illusion,
both habits to be broken.

Peter and Andrew debunked
my "strange ideas" and woman that I was,

I wept. Levi stepped in and calmed the others
the way the savior woke in the rocking

boat and calmed the sea. They all looked
at me in wonder. I spent the rest of my life

on earth infused with his apparition
because I knew that I was worthy.

II

Worlds

First Trip to the Infinite

Years before pop tops, I was five or six next to my brother
on a redwood bench. I held a can of orange soda
and looked through the triangle my Mother's church key bent.
I thought the spot of sun inside was a sailboat, loved
the traversing reflections, the zippity gleam, an enchanted door.

I think I willed myself to become abstract—
though I didn't know what that meant, it was the only way to enter.
I moved the can from angle to angle, followed the gold parallelogram
and again the triangle—crawled inside that vessel and traveled
from one orange shore to another, flew further and farther

to a region where light teemed forever
like the place where the fireflies we chased at dusk
were born. My eye on the flashes, little armadas
that couldn't sink in the ocean inside the aluminum walls
of the new world, I saw it was endless—

Not like the clothesline where my Mother stretched
her freckled arms. Not like the games the other kids played
till the sky went amethyst and their houses called from the mouths
of their doors. In the glimmering
sloop of the can, I abandoned my brother, forgot
my lavender sunsuit, my bare feet and braided hair—

For one long moment I coasted in the journeying bardo—lay down
in the curvature of the infinite
lit from within

like an orange is—circular, globular, spinning
to nothing, nothing
but center.

Early Childhood

Hardly a thing I can hold in my hand.
But I recall my small hand
on the polished mahogany table
out on the sun porch where I sometimes
napped on the day bed, my hand
like the pokey part of a compass
when I'd circle the table
for a small eternity each day, hand
holding steady, I'd hum to my parents'
songs as they rose from the monophonic
console: dawn in a one horse town,
the lowing of cattle, yodeling solos.
It wasn't the music that kept me
moving but my own hand mesmerizing
myself, barely tethered to earth beneath me
or the desert outside where heat blistered
my father's roses. Inside and above me,
my big parents came and went
like the sun that ladled its gold
on the tips of mountains, I had no words for
what lifted my vision there, groundless,
airy, clear—even then I leaned away
from the body's downward drop
where tears went when they fell
into dirt hidden by flowers where animal
bodies were buried. I knew *that* much—
I saw the Rangers shoot and shovel
under the coyote—so earth
wasn't comfort or warmth when I wanted
to purl my excursion into the music,
like the vapors of clouds, soaring
around the sky all day, nothing
to hold in my hand, just my hand
and those old songs,
circling lightly
in the dust on the table.

Swing

Small child obsessed with the swing, even in winter I'd go after
supper down to the basement, climb onto the wooden board tied to
the frayed ropes my father strung from the far-up rafters, the
insulated ceiling itself a place to reach for, to rise through—as I
kicked and counted, counted and kicked. I'd already learned that
numbers went always higher from zero to ten, to thirty, to eighty and

on and on all the way to one hundred which I mistakenly understood
as the lift off the cliff, the time to turn round, go back and begin
again, until one day my father explained: *one hundred and one, one
hundred and two, one hundred and* . . . I felt dizzy watching the digits fall
from his voice, fill the basement, then fly off my sneakers over those
rafters and out the roof to vanish on the horizon, and so I practiced

climbing the size of them, saw them ahead and ahead like infinite
Christmas lights or my parents' card, Doré's etchings of Dante's
paradise, rows of angels hand in hand in hand, carved in the
complicated heavens beyond human view, and I suffered a little
knowing the universe was that big, thinking I had to kick it open,
wing as high and as far as the numbers or angels, and still come back,

small hands calloused from holding the brown ropes, rough threads
of hemp, braided and knotted beneath my seat, as I bobbed over
lawn mower and gardening tools, as I listened for the furnace to kick
off and on, its heated thrum like a heart in synch with my own
rhythmic muscle. I kicked and counted the stairs to my mother's
kitchen, kicked and counted cinderblocks in the walls and the sway of

my sure young legs delivered me up and back, up and back over a
world, a circumference, my own planet holding steady, almost safe
beneath my butt as the minutes ticked and tumbled upon one
another until mother called me to rest for the night. Exhausted, I'd
stumble off of my swing lost in my sea legs, fingers, rashy and
swollen, I'd crawl up the seventeen stairs to my bath, my cinnamon
bear and bed—Another day older, another day counted and gone.

Self-Portrait With Parents

The yellow walls were gone.
Where it used to sing,
my room slammed shut.
In place of yellow, chocolate tones—my parents' words.
Mouths full of teeth, they beamed at me.
I was surprised, but not delighted
that they had painted my room.

Not happy enough
to make them happy,
under watchful eyes
I rocked in my little chair,
feeling the frequency
of the new color—Darker,
warmer, as if I'd moved

inland from shore,
under a tree from starry space.
I wanted to make myself
their candy-heart daughter.

I looked at the fluted skirt
on the dressing table,
the descent of spirals, new loops
of lace in the window.

Between that moment and the next,
I thought I've been here before—
felt myself grow sadder, older,

remembered how alone I was
being born.

Maybe The Flowers

spoke to me back then
when I picked those bouquets for my mother,
the incalculable summer of my yellow tutu.

       Barefoot, I leapt about
thinking myself some sort of pixie on the grass.
Maybe the flowers said not to grow up:

*You will worry about money, you will lose
yourself in vain men,
 cut off your hair. . . .*

       All Hallows Eve some pranksters
 burned two shrubs that framed our fieldstone path.
To reach the flowers again I had to pass

both bushes, now black as witches,
two fires in my head.   Finally,
the gardener dug them up and I crept back.

But the snapdragons looked dangerous,
the pansies were changelings, their eyes,
yellow slits. Even the roses were joyless,

persecuting the trellis, threading their thorns.
There was no happiness anymore. Nothing
looked pretty. And I forgot the flowers

ever talked. Silence grew wings
batting the morning air, stirring dried soil.
All of August on the swing set,

circling the toe of my sneaker
in desert sand, I watched fire ants
going in and out of a hole.

The Light That Gives Most Light

Sleeping late on Sunday after the film noir kept me
awake but still dreaming throughout the night. Choosing
from everything I can't have and never will, then
taking a favorite snack to the closet, licking vanilla
off my fingers while I sit on the floor among shoes
that can't walk me where I want to go. Stealing
from my best friend because she has too much, then
calling on God to forgive my stupid tears, calm
the trembling I promised I'd never feel in my fists.
And thanking the angels for the view from the pantry
window where I would go to write my songs, small songs
that gave me comfort when I was old enough to sense
the world careening out of control, though the light
still dawned inside me and fired my veins down
to the wrists like fuses for some ceremonious insight
awaited with patience, almost with pleasure.

What Keeps Us

When I recognized despair
for the first time, everything
went simple, everything
black or white. I looked up,
saw the whole sky, the
whole world clearly.
At three o'clock in the morning
I left the house, ran down the cul de sac
to the pond's rocks,
twisted my posture and crouched
in the back of the lot
like the mermaid statue I'd seen
in a *National Geographic.*

I couldn't go back,
couldn't bear
a home
distorted. I spoke
through the drizzle
of miserable tears
to the hedges and trees.
I gave up my complaint
to the night, a blot—
yet the light
began taking shape
and told me to wait—

until my father came
with gruff apologies
and shame
as we walked
over the dandelioned border
onto our sodded lawn.
My hand in his, I knew already
I'd lived too much. At thirteen,
I was prepared to die.
The flesh is nothing.
What keeps us is blood.

Where Vision Held

 From my window at the top of the stairs
I watched the small white van my mother privately
called turn into the driveway and douse its lights.

I heard scuffling, heard pleading and cursing,
creaked the door ajar, knelt on the landing. From my view
at the top of the stairs I watched three men subdue

my father into a hospital jacket. It was summer;
the lawns were too lavish, the willows, too full.
The sound of the van driven away

offered a dumb motor to memory, offered a silence
without relief. The bronze angel lamp on the breakfront
shone through its red shade, its batwing

shadow lofty over the bowl of fruit. That small red pool
of light gave me no comfort, but it was the haven
where vision held, where I perched, a young girl

on her knees looking down at the landing,
then up above it, my father's painting,
a black hooded figure on a hill.

The Hour Done

Death is the universal hydra for the imagination marked by water.
　　—Gaston Bachelard

You thread my body through the week's dreams,
skillfully sew into consciousness
the corpse of myself that I've supposedly outgrown.

So I'm to be grateful now, for nightmares?
When I awake alone, coughing and choking
to scan the hex of the hooded
furniture in the dark, I'll be shedding
the husk of my alien parts . . . ?

I refrain from complaining.
See my perfectly dead face in a hollow
of murky water, fish eyes open—*What could be worse?*
You say the dreams are ahead of me, in other words,
I died before my time to embody someone new.

The lonesome ghost of myself fills the room, hovers
above the wise bookcase, the vase of funereal gladiolus,
green as fog but transparent. Now it lumbers into your lap
wanting desperately to be named. I open my painted
mouth, pronounce an elegy for myself,

stutter for my father trying to suck him back—
How to grow a fresh incarnation under water?
One which gardens with eyes open.
A sentinel scouting the night

for the matter of a stray soul to root
and mate within the breathy greenhouse
of my body—The hour done,

I drive the winding country road, wondering
what wild vine is climbing behind the wheel.
I'm not what I used to be, not yet
what I'll become.

Kafka's Metamorphosis

When Greta plays the violin
for the three house guests,
beneath the kerosene lamps,
her music billows through the afterglow
of the evening meal. And the amber notes—
like trees inside tears, reach their branches

round the corner where Gregor nudges
his nostrils against the door,
lifting his carapace a few centimeters
into the corridor—he's dizzy
with enchantment, unaware
of losing the camouflage of walls,
almost human again
inside the waltz's folds,

and the boarders see the outrage,
the scaly torso staining the hall—
that's the saddest moment
of the story,
when he's utterly exposed
and disavowed by Greta
whom he adores hopelessly

now—Nothing left
for the final pages
but to be brutalized
and banished,
despised into death,
that's it.

Van Gogh's Room

Everyone's seen it. The wooden foot board
of the bed frame, slanted like the ceiling above

with the painting of a showgirl's golden hair
and his own self-portrait hung from wires.

The little table with blue pitcher and cruets
for vinegar or turpentine, and the mirror

that reflects nothing back. Tabula rasa
in a black frame. No wonder he sliced his ear,

jangled by interruptive smudges like these tan chips
across the sea-green floor. Blue door, closed, walls

with fauvist colors, even the green windows
bleed to a jaundiced yellow and hold no view.

All his monkish possessions in one cell
as if he could like Tarot's Fool step into unstirred

air, dance off a mountain to the tune he alone hears.
Thinking in those little wooden chairs. Their straw seats,

inverted Cezanne haystacks, snap my heartstrings.
But no one Vincent knows is here to share the sunlight

of Arles. Gauguin's already gone, burnt out in the islands
with the bronze Polynesian ladies draped in fuchsia

and lime sarongs. He'll lose a leg to gangrene,
forget Vincent completely, die leaving his paintings

and his notebook, never knowing *where we're going,
why we're here, from whence we've come—*

unlike Van Gogh who always knew.
Some never leave a room.

Gauguin's Red

after Museum notes, Museum of Fine Arts, Boston

Kerosene red of the 19th century
in the sculpted mantle to his hut. Scarlet
saris on the brown-skinned women,
of course. Terracotta dust he recalls from graves
in Pere La Chaise. Roses on the Left Bank, red
grillwork at a brasserie on Montparnasse.
Copper verdigris against a menstrual sunset.
Ominous red of mythic gods, the tongues of their lust,
their potent erections —primitive red

of his bloodshot eyes. Red scabs
on his gangrened foot. Syphilis-red. Red
of rolled tobacco and eucalyptus ash. Jasmine
on the Christian hillside where he was buried
in his thin red tie, his ruddy life a story
of not knowing *how to go, or when, or why* . . .
his pagan body lies beneath a crucifix against
blue sky, both putrefied and purified at once.

Sepia red. Voodoo red. Like the foxglove petals
his lover set on the headstone
to counterpoint that remorseless cross.

October Stars

There must be some wisdom in the drizzle
of these few October stars
or why would I turn night after night
to the cold floor of the back porch

after the neighbors' lights go out,
after the mother from the house next door
calls in Korean to her children
across the street—

where the night abandons the day's last cries
as the city grows its feral skin, reflected
in the ragged hair of that lone cloud
throwing itself across the moon

and October's orphaned stars
burn tears through the apron of black sky
as if to continue enduring their world, a world
already over, already eaten by its own fire,
moonless, motherless, gone—.

Paper Fan

Twilight on a night in May
and I'm holding the fan you made for me
on Mother's Day when you were six.

Twelve years it's lived on the far wall of my bedroom,
pinned like a wing behind the Polish marquetry,

and Aunt Adeline's Black Madonna
of Czestochowa draped in the Easter palms.

Popsicle handle. Five spidery-splayed
toothpicks hold the bowed fan in place.

I see the line your pencil drew which your scissors missed,
then your design brush-stroked on, Asian-ish, pinched pastels
in paper crepe glued randomly on spewed black ink.

It's Friday night—you've got your own spiffed-up car
and you're out with your favorite girl—last
hometown summer you surf the tide to a Freshman year.

I stroke my fingers across the fan and want to tell you now
what matters most is what you feel. How it's always
the difference of life or death.

I tuck the curved arch back behind Our Lady's mantle
while a chill belies the season. What we have left

 is innocence, the gold-inked edges
of this paper fan, incandescent behind the darkness.

It will be here when you visit.

Visual Ritual

Black winter nights
the heat rises
and the old windows rattle,
when I get into bed
under the stars
of my doubled quilts,
close my eyes and envision
the wealth of your hair, your
sweeping smile, the delicate inset
of bones, hands, as ever
in pockets, sweet
eyes, nose and mouth
your father passed down,

and I lift up my palms
and pull through my mind
the far spheres
that service this world,
pull a funnel of splendor,
sparkle and shimmer, flicker
and blaze, pull it down
in a vertical white figure eight,
pour it over your head,
then I orbit the circuits,
all boundaries subsumed
in one shielded zone,
crown, neck and shoulders,
chest, belly, buttocks,
thighs, knees and shins.
And ankles, and heels
in one spiral coil
lazered to dazzle—

the love of a mother
who from a distance
with this keeps you safe,
as she must
let you go.

The Worlds

Unwrap the bandage of your faith
and double it back over each fear.
You are loved beyond imagining
by the hum of one stone's existence.
against the many-stoned wall.

The light that airs your silhouette
beyond this little life sees through
the continent of time. Did you think
God would forget because you forgot?
How could perfection fail you?
How much you are a part of
him, me, it.

*

In my practice of quiet sitting, ichor
travels the body. The hand of the heart
extends like a lobsterman's net encompassing
everything and for a moment, everything
is under water, iridescent, holy. Silence

sings on the ceiling beam, ascends like smoke
through the roof. Minutes grow long.
A bat, a dragonfly, nothing—
Measure begins again.

*

I don't sleep when the town blackens.
Blurred doorways fire my eyelids,
No one is late for eternity.
I open the doors,
go in to my friends.

*

I've spent the night
with the world outside
inside, *the worlds—*.

"The Preponderance of the Small"

The Chinese Book of Changes said. And now
curious phenomena appear each time I forget where I am.
Chanterelles suddenly circle the lawn as if to remind me
of direction. The rain comes by, points to the crocuses' sorrow
and how I am wearing the wrong shoes. Or in the kitchen
a stray potato having fallen to the floor cries out like a cat
when I step on it. "Pay attention to little things"
the horoscope said, and just yesterday, the toothpaste spewed
an iridescent madonna, chartreuse sponge mold crept
over the clementines onto the drapes. And when I bent
to lace my boots, a cobwebbed cup of light dropped
into my face. For a moment I saw the plant's ferned imprint
in the bay window. Then one amber earring found
in the mandala of the Persian rug. Flying
buttresses in the shafts of the rattan chair .
Something's breathing at my back, organic
continuum underneath my nose. Acts
of living, symphonies which tiptoe
in my footsteps. High Mass
at home, the call to prayer.

The Bath Tub Is Optional

when you visit the meditation mansion
run by two retired nuns. One tiny cell of a room
with one tiny bed and an oval window, but oh,
beyond the window — wind and white caps, lips
of sand, lighthouse lording over the rocks.
Why would you want a bathtub when you could wash
yourself with the view? Clouds toweling the sunrise
emollient up to your elbows, between your thighs,
lavender light. And why would you want to bathe
the body you've trained as a transport for higher
beings to travel through? The busyness of quietude,
the eventually banished will, waftage of oxygen
pouring through pores, new atoms magnetized
till your chanting stills, though the spooks
warbling through your throat rewire you completely,
so you'll cry at nothing at all because everything matters

Down to Zero

We have no choice but to dance.

They dance in Pompeii, dance as the lava melts
the hill towns, rides roughshod over the homes.
Workers leave their markets, their gardens,

knot hands and dance over valleys and knolls
as in the last scene of Bergman's *Seven Seals*.
And lava seals. And burnt steel seals

like candlewax; it erupts, contorts and molds
into unexpected edges and petrifies
the people. Still, they dance

through the labyrinth, serpentine,
runny-rainbow, down to the zero
beneath, their steps out of synch.

Some throw back their heads to sing,
shut their eyes and leap up in their dancing
through sooty air looking for ledges

in clouds or in trees. Those far from the doors
dance through the tallest ceilings down
spiral stairwells from the towers.

They hold hands and jump.

III

Edens

Desire with Mountain and Dante

I am alone with the mountain and always
            desire, a wound
which opens as soon as it's healed

like those poor severed souls,
            Dante's Sowers of Discord, low
in the eighth circle. Alone
with the mountain, I contemplate
            the trembling ridge
                        where Lethe

washes the swollen tissue,
                memory of sin,
and I coax myself step
            after step, goat
hooves digging in
            to the sun-cusped
ganglia of rock, despair's
            dry valleys
within, and always desire
            against this white-
frocked sky, now under cloud-
            cover, now fully realized

in sequined star constellations,
miraculous planets and bird
            invocations—But what
does desire
            fulfill? *What*
                is it for?

    Bright feathered weight that I wear
            each day, alone
with the mountain
            or not—
                always there,
mountainous—
                is.

Only One Remark More

No opinions so strong they're strangled
by their own hard edges and get in our way.
Rather, something soft, a superfluity . . .

like Zinfandel in the tropics—Not zesty, not
eccentric, just a bottle in back of the fridge,
something peachy and already open—like that song

Friday night at the Karaoke, how it dolled up your tongue
to dapper, and there were no more remarks to reel in
for the rest of the evening—Super-fluidity

in your hands, your
fruity mouth on mine, so there were moans—
maybe, though I don't

remember them either—your fingers
entrained like birds
where I was the whole sky.

Mid-Morning

It was only a hug.
Out in public, no less.
But you were delicious.
The place where your
shoulder and neck come together,
the place where I rested my mouth
against your skin. Not exactly a kiss.
Just blotting my lipstick, really,
there—where there was no collar.
Just tee shirt and sweater and neck,
crinkles—freckles too . . . Well,
okay, a kiss. Maybe two. But small
and strewn like the leaves all over
the street, the ambers and reds.
And the brushing against. The
nudging and molding and
holding, like a dance without
feet. Only bodies and heads without
brains, or primitive brains
amid limbs. Count the arms
and the lips and the eyes and
the breath, and the width
of the warmth, and
the length and breadth
of everything
in between.

Accept the Anomaly

If you turn your back on the rent in your heart
you swallow the impossible, slam the brakes
on your circadian rhythms jarring hard circuitry
in your head. Like trying to prevent a paradigm shift—
stop Einstein from dwarfing Newton, for instance.

Eros is a disturbing anomaly. It won't fit your world view.
Before Copernicus, people thought the earth was still.
But you step off your porch into a cyclone with the one
Eros lashes you to—And it's dissonant music
you fall through, it's virtual, an altered state
where rules don't take, though chaos isn't what we think—

There's silent white space in the center where all forms
potentiate within God.   Accept the anomaly.
This isn't simple. But you can't lose or refuse what's yours.
Unless you enter the rent in the heart of your heart,
you won't fully know what you are.

I Was Looking Into Your Eye

looking into the tight skein of skin around
your eye, the folds, a flake, a freckle, that fiftyish
shift in the crows' feet, expanding bends and dents
and shadowed gutters—then back to the rich copper,
denuded eye, without the frame of its usual lens.
How vulnerable it is, more so than from a distance
when you are handsome and pensive, a bit out of focus.
In the loft of your cheekbone, the mottled sun-
spanked skin, pulled at an intersection of pigment
and damage. And your blink, the animal caged
under scope, shrunken pupil, widened iris ,
that driven quest up a mountain top to
God. I loved it! That will to keep looking,
to keep looking for—.

When He Said

When he didn't say. When he left the—
when he took the—when he hung up.
When he called. When he drove the,
drove the, drove the—when he parked.
When he looked that way. When he looked
away. When he didn't. When he wrote,
when he didn't write back—When
he paid. When he didn't pay. When
he didn't tip! When he bought the, when he
brought the, when he didn't bring the,
when he forgot . . . When he promised.
When he wanted, when he admitted
that he wanted. When he slept,
when he couldn't sleep
over. When he left. When he answered
back. When he laughed at—
when he spoke so loud, when he
whispered . . . oh, when he whispered . . .
When he sang to me, when he hissed,
when he pissed me off—When he wept
and when he walked away. When he crossed
the street that time to hide, and that other time—
when he slammed the—, when he
damned it all. When he kicked the—
when he broke the—When he always,
when he almost, when he never. When
I wouldn't. When he couldn't.
When we did.

Original Human

The fable attributed to Aristophanes in the Symposium . . . human beings
were ovoid-shaped doubles who became severed in two by Zeus
as a punishment when they revolted against the gods.
                                        —Veronika Goodchild

We simply can't stand up, our faces two red berries
glazed together, still damp after love. The way my right eye
studies your left, lines at the temples grinning also. The way
our noses rub like sniffing pups and how my mouth
keeps lolling open, as if to inhale the whole room,

blanket, pillows, sheets, your ear lobe, tongue—world
converted at noon, office to bedroom. And we are hungry
well past lunch, organic tendrils, persimmon, pomegranate, plum—
I liked how he called what we did "deep kissing,"
as if it qualified for the Olympics. I loved how we
rocketed into one comfortable animal on the floor cushions,

that close, like Plato's original human.
Did we reach the soul we share? Did it murmur
before it bellowed like a comet inside us—And how often
will we bring our flock of appendages back?

Like moths sucking up to summer doorways, lamplit
in darkness, pull of moonshine on water, megalithic
wand sparking the sea, hurling curves
of that joint body, Platonic pattern in motion
finding form like this and finally unafraid to drown.

White Tee Shirt

I was swimming in your skin—under
your neck and chest—but when you left the room
for a moment, I shoved my nose into your tee shirt
on the quilt and there was still more of you there,

more savory scent in the plain white cotton
in which I steeped my head, a wonder
I'd never dare to pray for—though I could
worship that crumpled complement like a relic

even as I flung it over the rocking chair.
You returned then and we carried on
while I thought about your shirt, peculiarities
that people fall in love with, distinguished

twine of DNA, sinuous helix of what we are
to each other, wrapped tight or shed
and gathered back—to help us recognize
again the way we live as separate creatures.

Hair By Hair

He said "We need to proceed word by word
hair by hair." And these admonitions frightened her.
She didn't want to proceed; she wanted to stop,
or rather, go back to where it was before
it went haywire. But there was Time
wearing its black raincoat, tapping its foot
at the edge of the hill. She could have shot it
dead. She could have laminated its silhouette
and locked it in a closet to remind her
there had been a moment, a white one,
one like a braided shawl on her shoulders
where fond fingers touched her as if she were part
of another, part of a plan of naked intentions
rainbowed by sun falling through water
under his outdoor shower with the old oilcloth
curtain, dopey cows prowling beyond the fence,
and the reptilian face of the rooster telling her
the future would always be late.

The Chaotic Pendulum

in this museum looks like a relationship to me.
One reaction, one abreaction. But I think we
are more like this Tri-Zonal Space-Warper,
responding to illusion, where something
looks like it's moving when it's not.
Like we need these 3-D glasses to see

that rocket shot up to Mars to show scientists
in Houston there really was water once in these craters.
That project was christened "Endurance . . . "
not unlike ours, though we don't proceed at 27 times
the speed of sound, but suffer beneath florescent
lights awaiting the Vast Awareness to pass through us.

Like when I say "Let's take it to the next level"
and you say *"Whaa . . . ?"* Or I say
 "We are so over!" And you say" *Whaa . . . ?"*
And the Coriolas Effect bearing down on a plane
where wind and ocean currents curve
is something like love, time and other miscellany

expanding or contracting depending
upon how close together bodies are.
Sometimes there's disconnected resonance
more serious than this Hyperbolic Paraboloid
when we bow like this rod to slip through
one another's hang-ups . Or when we attempt

Virtual Volleyball as if we were on some reality show
where the stakes are fortune or death . . .
How we drive and ride one another's
sensors—all lights and circuit-breakers,
dials and knobs, positrons, negatrons—

making our own human battery.

Crow

I dithered in the Radisson Hotel room listening
to the big Wyoming wind. No tree branches to hold
the roaring. I couldn't look at the phone.
Beneath the howl I heard a
Resurrection choir, some high-pitched miracle
of voices—I knew it was crazy, I was crazy—
my ears buzzed from the
flight and the spirits moved
in, big-throated angels cushioned my chest. I
ignored them—couldn't look
at the phone. Couldn't find my rental car key
or the credit card thing to get back in the door
when I went out. I had to go out
soon, had to lead some seminar but couldn't
find a blank piece of paper to
scratch my notes. Stacks of books and
Xeroxed hand-outs all over the beds. I had a list.
I'd lost the list. Tiny post-its flew like
yellow tumbleweeds from my hands
which shook as I shook out my
clothes, brushfire bedcovers on the carpet.
I couldn't look
at the phone. I thought, or tried to think,
idiot chemistry racing from
temple to temple to heart—that
squawking starving crow,
my stupid heart.

Final Longitude

There are broken rosaries in my dreams.
We are up to our knees in murky water and the rain
has been poisoned, sallowing our skin with pesticides.
All your life you've been immunized from risk, waiting
for the roof to fall. Listen, it's possible the past will always
carry its cross uphill and the future is just a phantom

in an evening dress seen through stained glass.
No doorbell, no mail slot will let her in. The truth is
you have only these small moments fallen in your lap,
swarms of fireflies you've brushed aside without notice.
It is time now to take the measure of their wings. Time
to realize we are blessed with an aria only the two of us
can sing. I want us to call out each other's names
in the wind that never stops messing up our hair,

our clothes. Let's remember flesh coming together,
what it is that humans do mixing their limbs, how
a man dips into a woman in a room lit by touch, and sunlight
shifts through curtains where the pattern is latticed
so even the shadows on the ceiling climb out
of their bodies, above gravity and time.
Can't you feel the fear again tonight on the evening news

warning us not to trust the streets. Not to reach
for the healing lotion of another's arms
without some notarized adherence to the rules.
Fine print is full of bars in the jails
we are taught to believe in. I am weary
of elusive words and wary of a world that doesn't
want my miracles. There is a border to the territory
of you, a final longitude and I am headed there.

My Heart in the Witness Protection Program

I was afraid they'd off me, those crooks
whose sordid business I'd exposed at the televised trial.
My heart was pretty darn sad to pack everything up
and leave Massachusetts for that desiccated land
where language was flat as the side of a semi,

for that suburbia of ordinaries
stepping out of their houses each morning
still in pajamas to pick up the paper before the loose dogs
pissed on the headlines. And yes, my heart missed the comfort

of New England trees, avuncular oaks, assorted canopies
of green, and it winced a little each day as we drove
my witness-protected Toyota down to the canyon KMart
where we could wander the aisles like nobodies,
not pink and contused, not bleeding between the steel slats
of the shopping cart. Not even screaming at sticks staked

through the soil of discounted plants as we walked
among the appliances, cusinarts with seven situational
speeds for chopping and crushing, mincing and flaying,
for slapping and stabbing and mutilating—Do I need
to say my heart wasn't happy in that arid little Gulag?

But weeks rolled into months as we played Black Jack
on Friday nights with other meat-stained tattlers and killers,
thieves and thugs who lived down the avenue, and like anyone's
heart, mine acclimated to that contaminated little town . . .

through all the black heavens scorched starless—
with their twisted, their listing, their skinny, balsamic moons.

L'Arch de Triomphe

And when it cracks—
the whole stance of the heart
yaws in the chest, small Titanic
heaving —and the rest of the body knows
all sustenance is useless. Flatlined,
the heart won't feed like a school of fish.

Instead it makes the sound
politicians don't ever talk about when wallets flash
and they're caught taking bribes. So the heart too
has its Mafioso side, its dishonorable discharge,
legs and torso on the steps, upper body askew
in the gutter like Jimmy Cagney
in *Public Enemy.*

There's an old Italian saying
Ifa you sing, the pain goesa 'way!
And so from the gorge in its bosom, the heart
belts a few notes like Edith Piaf in the subway,
bony knees beneath bony coat, frail
little sparrow—*Je Ne Regrette Rien*—

insufferable song of survival
in a minor key which only the wounded
hear from their compact cars
chaotically swerving in drunken traffic
around Place d'Etoile, honking the naked
horns of their hearts under the Arch
de Triomphe—in Paris,
the city of *love.*

Mystique

We survived
the blast, the reek of burnt
cabbage, putrid clouds, closer
than we suspected.
Your ears

went inside out. My hair blew
off. A phone rang
in a cemetery. People kissed
thorns and strangled
roses, dread
instead of buds
in the branches—

Because a dream seeped
from the factory and fell
through the chainlink
fence, your breath, residue
of celestial treble—mute
as you held back

your pale mystique, your
weak eyes that see the world
from its first day. Still
we were alive, treads
of your boots wrenched
from deeper shadows, though
there were codes to decipher,
pages strewn over tombs, no

lexicon to consult
but one slap of moonlight
which spelled

the one word we knew
in that country, that impossible
language.

Inside Light

Within each cell there are little and littler parts.
The way you imagine water droplets in meditation
while breathing through your eyelids so as
to harness the codes of light. Light grows
inside cells, glows in the body through corpuscles

in the blood. That's what life is—
luster, patina, scintilla and shine . . .
When the glowing stops, you're dead!
But how to keep the circuit bright till then?
This is the question you ask, drying your hair

each morning before the foggy mirror where
eyes perceive color and nerves send tracers
infinitesimal times a second, prying open
the spectrum inside your mind, projecting it
onto the world—We all live inside light.

The moon and stars are within us—that's
consciousness, God's first idea. And His second?
Eros, of course, candlelight, fireworks, blown
fuses, darkness in the back room where
the rest of his tricky moves take place.

Tree

Perhaps it is in this tree. Perhaps
the wholeness she seeks only needs
her perception to seize it,
tracing the tar of the driveway
stepping into the maple.

The tree bends over the road
and never goes anywhere,
appeased with a sky
and complementary color.

Bared to the breeze, the tree
doesn't brace for the wind, but takes it
into its spaces. Lets storm shuffle
foreign arrows through interstices
between leaves. When winter comes,

as it does, the tree expects it,
is proper in mourning,
slowly withering brilliance
before the chilled armor of air.

In the deep fur of its freezing,
the tree straightens what muscles contract,
though it doesn't promise deliverance
much less a future of blossoms.
Yes, the tree says, *winter is here
and winter is perfect.*

Even the woman who's scattered her roots
must cook herself dinner.
Under the window's branched shadow,
she invites the tree to the table.

In the dusk of its arms
she lights a candle,
how she loves
what it does to the room.

I Am, I Will

No pastries for breakfast, just a pear in my pocket and a long walk
on the beach at 6 a.m., wearing my bullet-proof bra and grey
duster as in an old film noir. Now the sun
lifts quickly from its bed of waves, like the pink
rubber handball from junior high school, compact
disc ejected from the horizon. The sea is muted,

understated in steady breakers. *I Am, I Will,*
says the sun and *Let it be.* And I do
not think of you as I watch gulls cross the sun
in formation like planes at the air show. And I think of how
it took guts to play handball with the guys when I was twelve.
I think *Top Gun*—and how these birds are perfectly aligned.
Then when the lead flaps his wings, his side-kick pulses

till they're all in synch and cease their flutter at once
to dive through the reddened edges of sun which begin to yellow
as if another sun lay behind them. The few clouds are doused
in raiment. And the disc burns, unconsumed, like Moses' bush
while some god turns and awakens from sleep

so the light deepens. I stare, then stare at after-images
everywhere, the unconscious issue of the sun assaulting
both sand and sky, how it abides as whole civilizations are lost
and gone. I think of Shelley's *Ozymandias,*
how even things meant for endurance
crumble and die. And I think of the Buddha

and his one revelation, *everything changes.*
I do not think of us as a lone surfer jogs by, his board
so much lighter than a cross beneath his buffed arm,
his wetsuit zipped up snug so within his rubber skin
the bone-chilling water will warm
and will keep him
warm.

Dusk

Futile
to speak of us now
that we are erased. Your name
as if it lived under moon rock,
frostbitten. Even in the bullet holes
of my complaints, all is
unutterable. Yesterday I wanted
to erect a memorial. Post photos amongst
bees and weeds at the beach that no longer
castles my life.   I chose instead to watch a few
disassembling clouds slim into spirals
and fade where the hearth
of dusk is hidden. The moon's dark
side begs for navigation
like a psychomantium where a spirit
is held. One beam rubs
light beside the vase's shadow
where I've placed white camellias
on the table's white doily,
as if moonlight and fresh flowers
could bring me home
consoled.

This Morning From The Porch

Unbearable brilliance.   Each leaf surrendering
to the late ceremony of sun. The neighbor's tomato plants
have fallen through the slats in the white fence
and in the breeze, there's no denying autumn.
I keep my windows open despite the chill.

This afternoon I read how Blake thought man was bound
to the worm since God created Adam from clay and earth.
His painting shows Elohim's hands on Adam's head,
both their expressions, contorted and tormented.

From across the street tonight a child hollers twenty times
Nobody likes me, Nobody likes me—All day I have not spoken,
so I call from my window *I do, I do!*   Though I'm not sure
which child it is that cried or for how long I could abide him.

I think of Blake's red color print, the huge serpent
wound around Adam's legs. Creation then, is spirit
trapped in form, the first stage of the fall.

When the lousy movie on TV ends with a brutal death,
I stand by the window weeping into the cicadas.
Something palpable rises and multiplies in the darkness.
Free-floating between breaths, it deepens down to the worm.

I remember Adam's dark red fruit, the struggle up from mud.
I cry for summer's end and for the child no one likes.
For humankind and the green world's serpents.
I am crying because I cannot bear imagining more love.

Fallen

Here—I have fallen in love with pastel silhouettes
and a carob tree and the lights across the canal. I have fallen
in love with the gentle gloaming, the scent of mimosas,
tropical skies. Fallen for the warm wind inside
the thousand thread count of the clouds. I have fallen for fog
around two palm trees on the public beach at dawn
and the stones between them where I place my chair.
And I love the quiet of faraway cruise ships, the intimate
shimmer of rose shadows at dusk. My rituals in moonlight.
Still, I don't know what I'm meant to relinquish
into the blue trumpet flowers and climbing asters that languish
above the overgrown roots of banyans. As I conjure a spell
from locked spirals inside the coral, as I honor sweet seeds
in their fullness, I can't understand for the life of me how
I have fallen this long way south with my useless love . . .
But I have fallen in love again with Rumi's Beloved within, Fromm's
love as an Act of Will, Socrates' Human Agape—and the practice
of keeping my own theories close with their memories
of limerance and pheromones.

Early

The quiet has its breath and the sea breathes me.
Today the strange sun, sunken in fog, its fuchsia
held still by violet haze. Solitary

circle, smooth and solid as a pocket
stone. I come early to the public beach
before the quiet collapses in the crowd

of voices. The sun breathes me
too. I am kept living by their living, sea and sun.
I'm kept alive by constancy. I count

on the sea's counting, its
syncopations. I am danced by exhalations
in white crests. Wandering, I come on the scrim

by way of the sea's surface, starry reflections
where my recesses are lit from within. I am surprised
to find my feet, lost in last night's dream.

I splash my applause for the sea and sun, plough
my feet in sand. Too soon I will be sand
myself, kept alive by damp creatures

since sand breathes water, so life
is there also. Then even death is life, death
dreamed by sun and sea, who also dream me

in the mornings when I come
to the early scrim
of light.

Moment

It was quiet on the bed. My eyelids drenched
with presence. The air was more than there,

more than space. I watched the lace curtain smooth itself
into the oval window's dusk. There were no

contradictions. This was a knowing
in the dimensions of the ceiling, the pressure

of the fan. Paradox whose message
is grace. I could have bathed in its folds

the way nightfall smolders into dawn. No need
to wrap the room's perimeter of sin

around my shoulder. No perimeter
at all—a music, more than

air, the essence here
on earth. The ladybug crawled

across the quilt as if she cherished
every inch of her pilgrimage

from the garnet square to blue.
It was time to fly and time to be

still within the white noises
whose cadences were waves

of lace which met my eyes
upon opening, my eyes

in synch inside the mind's
unbidden whisper:

See, *all is new.*

Last Words

There is no more to be taught.
No more to be taken
away. Loss is the same
as less. A small idea

of the mind in a polarized universe.
I can be naked in rage or naked in
knowledge. Though my pajamas
are torn, I can still sleep.

Despair is a deadly sin
but not surrender.
Though you may think
you're no longer protected,

you can hold more,
if you open your arms.

Notes

The Gospel of Mary & Magdalen The Nag Hammadi Library, also known as
the Gnostic Gospels, was discovered in 1947. It includes many gospels, such
as the famous Gospel of Thomas, which were ruled unauthorized by the
council of Nicea in the 4th century. Much of Mary's gospel did not survive
and some of it is in fragments. Rilke's poem The Egyptian Mary is also
about St. Mary Magdalene as inspired by The Golden Legend. She is
worshipped all over France as a teacher and is often shown with a book and a
skull in her hands. According to the Golden Legend, written in 1265 by the
Dominican Archbishop of Genoa, Jocabus da Voragine, Marseilles was the
place of many Magdalene miracles and Mary, the widow of Christ, came to
Marseilles, an active port at the time, in France or Gaul, as it was called then,
with her siblings, Martha and Lazarus. These stories have been repressed by
the Roman Church which sanctioned only four of the many gospels to be
part of its canon. She is associated with the grail "vessel" in the heresies.

Bronze Goddess Speaks was inspired by a statue representing Sequana from the
Gallo-Romain epoch found at one of the springs of the Seine River over
which a Christian sanctuary was built. Many of the 200 or so black
madonnas or "vierges noirs" in France have also been dug up near wells and
springs on the locations of Gothic churches.

Rouen 1431 After a bogus trial, Joan of Arc was incarcerated and executed
in Rouen, France.

Tarot & Tuesday Night With the I Ching Both the Fool and the Hanging Man in
Tarot and the hexagram "Deliverance" in the *I Ching,* or *Chinese Book of
Changes,* have to do with changing perspective and surrender to an alignment
with the Tao or will of the universe.

Last Judgment This poem borrows its structure from Rilke's poem by the
same name published in English as *New Poems* (1908) *The Other Part* translated
by Edward Snow. This poem, *Eve, Eons After,* and *The Gospel of Mary* all
subscribe to universal occult teachings and *A Course in Miracle* which sees our
world as an illusion created by our thoughts.

*The last three words of *Moment* are from St. John's *Revelation.*

Deborah DeNicola's spiritual memoir *The Future That Brought Her Here: Memoir of a Call to Awaken,* was released in 2009 from Nicholas Hays/Ibis Press. She is the author of *Where Divinity Begins* (Alice James Books, 2002) and four chapbooks. DeNicola edited the anthology *Orpheus & Company; Contemporary Poems on Greek Mythology* from the University Press of New England. Among many awards, Deborah has received an NEA Fellowship. Her poetry is published widely in journals and online. Her web site is www.intuitivegateways.com.

CPSIA information can be obtained at www.ICGtesting.com
Printed in the USA
LVOW082157111212

311079LV00003B/206/P